Fact Finders®

WHAT YOU NEED TO KNOW ABOUT
MENINGITIS

RENEE GRAY-WILBURN

CONSULTANT:
DR MARJORIE J. HOGAN

raintree

a Capstone company — publishers for children

Raintree is an imprint of Capstone Global Library Limited, a company incorporated in England and Wales having its registered office at 7 Pilgrim Street, London, EC4V 6LB – Registered company number: 6695582

www.raintree.co.uk
myorders@raintree.co.uk

Developed and Produced for Raintree by Focus Strategic Communications, Inc.
Adrianna Edwards: project manager
Ron Edwards: editor
Rob Scanlan: designer and compositor
Mary Rose MacLachlan: media researcher
Francine Geraci: copy editor and proofreader
Wendy Scavuzzo: fact checker

Printed and bound in China.
ISBN 978 1 474 70399 4
19 18 17 16 15
10 9 8 7 6 5 4 3 2 1

British Library Cataloguing in Publication Data
A full catalogue record for this book is available from the British Library.

Photo Credits
Alamy: David Hoffman Photo Library, 14, Mediscan, 29, Nucleus Medical Art Inc, 17, Radius Images, 15; Centers for Disease Control and Prevention, 25; Glow Images: Corbis/Jose Luis Pelaez, 26; iStockphoto: PicturePartners, 27, Shantell, 12; Library of Congress, 7; Science Source: Alfred Pasieka, 22, BSIP, 28, Evan Oto, 4, Jim Dowdalls, 10, Reed Business Publishing/Andrew Bezear, 11, Royal Victoria Infirmary, Newcastle upon Tyne/Simon Fraser, 5, SPL, cover (bottom); Shutterstock: A and N Photography, 13, Canit, 23 (bottom), Dziewul, 18, everything possible (background), back cover and throughout, GeorgeMPhotography, cover (top), 1 (top), hxdbzxy, 24, Ilike, 16, Sebastian Kaulitzki, 1 (bottom) and throughout, 8, 20, tab62, 19; SuperStock: Exactostock/George Doyle, 23 (top); U.S. National Library of Medicine, 6

Every effort has been made to contact copyright holders of material reproduced in this book. Any omissions will be rectified in subsequent printings if notice is given to the publisher.

All the internet addresses (URLs) given in this book were valid at the time of going to press. However, due to the dynamic nature of the internet, some addresses may have changed, or sites may have changed or ceased to exist since publication. While the author and publisher regret any inconvenience this may cause readers, no responsibility for any such changes can be accepted by either the author or the publisher.

CONTENTS

CHAPTER 1
WHAT IS MENINGITIS?

"It feels like a bomb going off in my head!" That is how 15-year-old David described the pain to his doctor. The doctor examined David. Then he told him he had a disease called meningitis. Meningitis is an infection of the **meninges**. These tissues swell when they are infected. David had pain in his head and neck. This was caused by the swollen meninges squeezing against his brain and spinal cord.

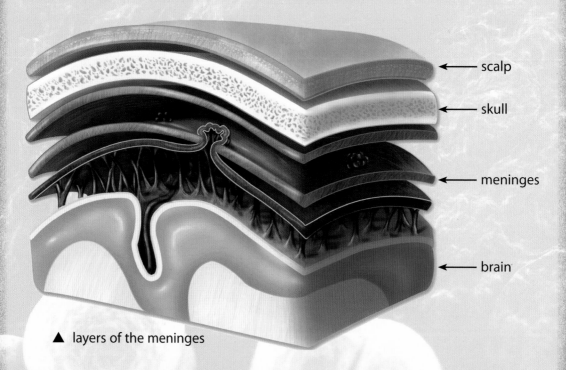

scalp

skull

meninges

brain

▲ layers of the meninges

meninges three layers of tissue that surround the brain and spinal cord

David's brain tissue swelled so much that his body could not work properly. He could not get out of bed, eat solid food or see very well. After many days of tests and treatment, David finally started to get better. He spent 15 days in hospital. Then he spent another month resting at home. This helped David to recover.

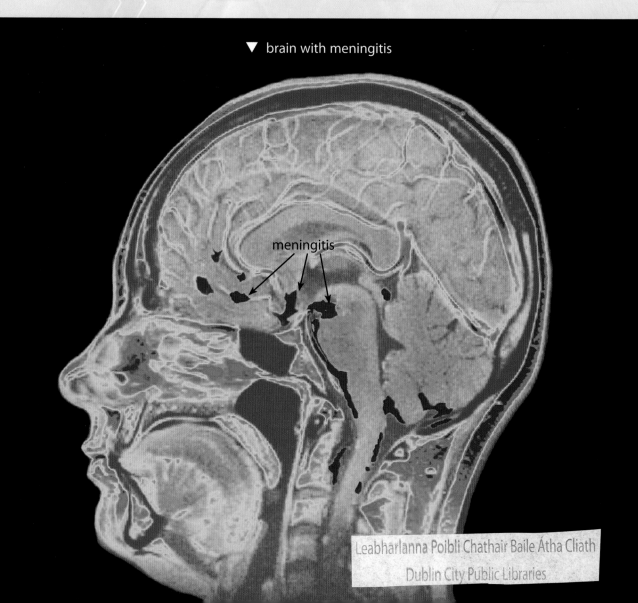

▼ brain with meningitis

meningitis

HISTORY OF MENINGITIS

The first recorded case of meningitis was in 1805. That was the year an **outbreak** of meningitis occurred in a village in Geneva, Switzerland. Thirty-three people died.

Meningitis was once called brain fever. No one knew what caused this disease. Then, in 1887, Anton Weichselbaum, an Austrian scientist, made a discovery. He found that a type of **bacteria** could cause meningitis. About 20 years later, US scientist Simon Flexner made a medicine from the blood of horses. This medicine kept many people from dying of meningitis. In the mid-1940s doctors used a new **antibiotic** called penicillin to treat meningitis. Forms of penicillin are still used today in treating the disease.

▲ Anton Weichselbaum

▼ Simon Flexner

TIMELINE OF MENINGITIS

1805	first medical record of meningitis by Swiss doctor Gaspard Vieusseux
1887	Dr Anton Weichselbaum discovers bacteria that causes meningitis
1891	Heinrich Quincke uses first spinal tap to test spinal fluid for meningitis bacteria
1905	major meningitis epidemic in Africa, killing thousands of people
1905–07	US scientist Simon Flexner develops a medicine from horses to kill meningitis bacteria
1928	Alexander Fleming discovers penicillin, the world's first antibiotic
1944	first successful use of penicillin in treating meningitis
1974	first vaccine for meningitis is approved
1996–2007	more than 20,000 die from meningitis outbreak in Africa
2005–10	additional vaccines are licensed to protect against four of five major meningitis-causing bacteria

▶ Alexander Fleming

outbreak when a number of people become ill at the same time from the same germ source

bacteria one-celled, microscopic living things that exist all around you and inside you; many bacteria are useful, but some cause disease

antibiotic drug that kills bacteria and is used to cure infections and disease

TYPES OF MENINGITIS

There are five main types of meningitis: viral, bacterial, fungal, parasitic and **non-infectious**. Meningitis that is caused by a **fungus** or a **parasite** cannot be spread from person to person. The same is true of non-infectious meningitis. Only meningitis caused by a **virus** or bacteria can spread from person to person.

VIRAL MENINGITIS

Viral meningitis is the most common type. This is a serious illness, but it is not usually deadly. The virus is spread through sneezing, coughing, sharing saliva or contact with unwashed hands after going to the toilet.

Having the virus does not mean that you will get meningitis. Meningitis happens only when the virus infects the meninges cells. Children under five years old and others with weak **immune systems** have the greatest chance of getting viral meningitis.

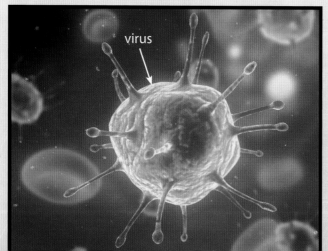

virus

◀ virus

Can meningitis spread from person to person?

viral ⟶ yes
bacterial ⟶ yes
fungal ⟶ no
parasitic ⟶ no
non-infectious ⟶ no

MENINGITIS

Type	Cause	How do you get it?
Viral	Virus that infects the meninges	A meningitis-causing virus can enter the body through an infected person's sneeze or cough.
Bacterial	Bacteria that infect the meninges	By having very close contact with an infected person for an extended period of time, such as sharing a bedroom
Fungal	Fungus that spreads from a person's bloodstream into the spinal cord	By taking certain medicines that weaken the immune system or by inhaling fungal spores of bird droppings found in the soil
Parasitic	A parasite found in warm bodies of fresh water, such as lakes and rivers, swimming pools, etc.	A parasite can enter through a person's nose and travel up into the brain.
Non-infectious	Head injuries, certain medications, some cancers and brain surgery	Many other causes, besides infection, can result in swelling of the meninges.

non-infectious illness or disease not caused by germs

fungus single-celled organism that lives by breaking down and absorbing the natural material it lives in

parasite animal or plant that lives on or inside another animal or plant and causes harm

virus germ that infects living things and causes diseases

immune system part of the body that protects against germs and diseases

BACTERIAL MENINGITIS

Bacterial meningitis is rare. But it is the most dangerous type of meningitis. Its **symptoms** come on suddenly. The disease may cause serious problems. It can even cause death if it is not treated in time. Bacterial meningitis is a type that can cause outbreaks.

symptom sign that suggests a person is ill or has a health problem

▼ Bacteria attack the meninges tissues.

Just like viruses that cause meningitis, bacteria can spread from person to person. Healthy people can have meningitis-causing bacteria in their noses or throats without becoming ill. These people are called carriers. But if a person's immune system is weak, it may not be able to fight off the bacteria. If bacteria reach the meninges, then meningitis could result.

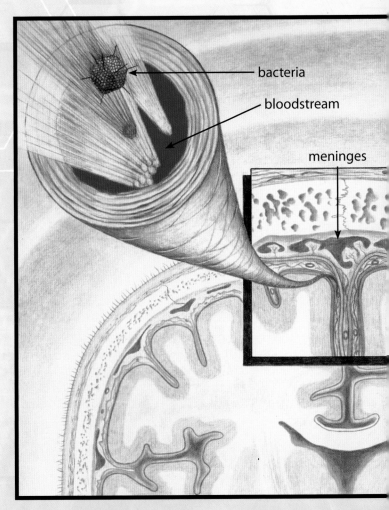

bacteria

bloodstream

meninges

▶ Meningitis-causing bacteria travel from an infection in the body, through the bloodstream, and to the meninges.

HEALTH FACTS

- In the early 1900s 75 to 80 per cent of people who had meningitis died.
- On average, there are about 3,200 cases of bacterial meningitis every year in the UK.
- Numbers of people with bacterial meningitis in the UK have fallen by half since 1990.
- About 20 per cent of people who get bacterial meningitis are between 11 and 24 years old.

CHAPTER 2

SYMPTOMS OF MENINGITIS

Have you ever had flu? If so, you probably remember having a fever, headache, sore muscles and perhaps nausea. Meningitis patients can have these same symptoms. But there are big differences between flu and meningitis. Both illnesses can cause headaches. But most people with meningitis describe that headache as the worst they ever had.

▲ If you have aches and a fever, staying in bed is a good idea.

Meningitis can make light hurt the eyes. It can also cause rashes or bruises.

A person with meningitis may have only some of these symptoms. And the symptoms of bacterial and viral meningitis look and feel the same. The only way to diagnose the disease is through lab tests.

HEALTH FACT

Flu can make you ache all over. But with meningitis, patients usually feel severe pain in the neck and sometimes in the back.

▼ lab testing for meningitis

NICHOLAS' STORY

One day when Nicholas was eight years old, he felt very sick. He had a bad headache, stomach pain and started coughing a lot. Sometimes he vomited when he coughed. His mum took him to hospital. They sent him home, saying it was just flu. But overnight, Nicholas got much worse. The tiniest bit of light hurt his eyes. And the lightest touch or breeze on his legs caused pain all the way up his back. It felt like someone was stabbing him.

He went back to hospital. The doctors put a long needle in his spine to pull out fluid. The fluid was supposed to be clear. But Nicholas' was so cloudy it was almost a solid colour. The doctors said he had bacterial meningitis. They started giving him medicine through a tube in his arm to kill the infection.

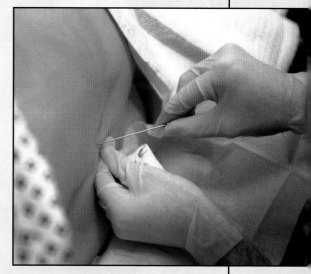

▲ testing for meningitis by pulling out fluid from the spine

Nicholas was in hospital for a week. After he went home, it took another week until he was able to walk on his own again. Although this happened over 10 years ago, Nicholas still gets pain in his back because of the meningitis.

HOW ARE THEY DIFFERENT?

Disease	Symptoms
Flu	Fever/chills, cough, sore throat, runny or stuffy nose, muscle or body aches, headache, feeling tired, vomiting
Viral meningitis	High fever, severe headache, stiff neck, **seizures**, sensitivity to bright light, sleepiness or trouble waking up, nausea/vomiting, lack of appetite, lack of energy
Bacterial meningitis	Fever and chills, changes in behaviour (such as confusion), severe headache, stiff neck, seizures, sensitivity to bright light, sleepiness or trouble waking up, nausea/vomiting, small red marks on the skin (severe cases)

▶ Some symptoms of flu are similar to symptoms of meningitis.

seizure sudden attack of illness caused by brain swelling or other symptoms; also called a convulsion

TESTING FOR MENINGITIS

If you have symptoms of meningitis, a doctor will order laboratory tests to confirm the diagnosis. The tests may include a CT/CAT scan. This is a special X-ray that creates 3-D pictures of the body or its organs. Doctors will also take samples of your blood, urine and spinal fluid. They may also take a saliva sample from your throat to check for any meningitis-causing bacteria.

These tests show what type of meningitis a person has. They can also identify the type of virus or bacteria causing it. This is important information to help doctors decide how to treat it.

▼ taking a saliva sample to test for meningitis

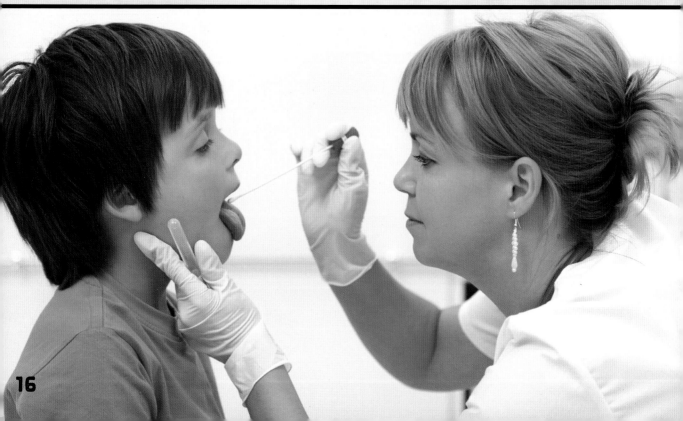

SPINAL TAP

To test for meningitis, doctors take fluid from the spine. This is called a spinal tap. First they numb the area near the bottom of the spine using a painkilling drug. Then they insert a long needle into the spinal cord. They withdraw some spinal fluid. Healthy fluid is clear. Fluid containing meningitis bacteria is cloudy.

▼ how a spinal tap works

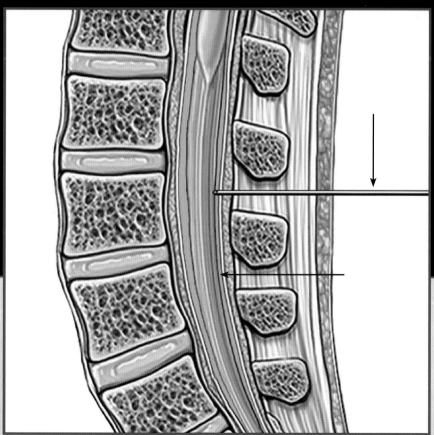

CHAPTER 3

HOW IS IT TREATED?

Test results show what type of meningitis a person has. But doctors give the patient antibiotics straight away, before the results come in. This helps stop any possible bacterial infections. A tube with a needle is placed into a vein in the hand, arm or chest. This mean that the antibiotics can go directly into the patient's bloodstream.

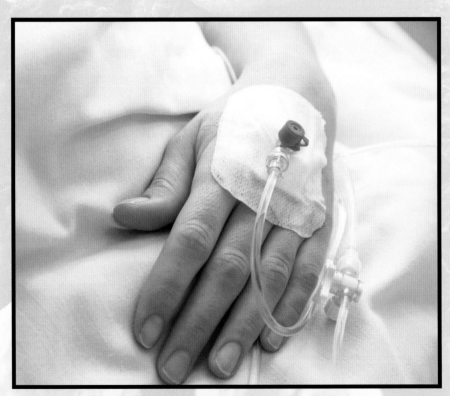

▲ Antibiotics enter the bloodstream through a tube and needle.

VIRAL MENINGITIS

If the tests show viral meningitis, antibiotics are stopped because they do not work on viruses. Medicine that attacks specific viruses may be given instead.

Most patients with viral meningitis get better on their own in one or two weeks. They may not even need to stay in hospital. Most just need plenty of rest, fluids and medicine for pain. They can recover fully, with no lasting problems. Other people may continue to have headaches, tiredness and memory loss from viral meningitis.

▼ It is important to drink a lot of water when recovering from meningitis.

BACTERIAL MENINGITIS

People with bacterial meningitis usually stay in hospital for a week or longer. They continue to receive antibiotics while doctors watch for other symptoms. These can include swelling in the brain, **shock** and seizures.

Bacterial meningitis has many possible after-effects. Some are not too serious, such as headaches, sore muscles, weakness and poor appetite. Other effects can last a long time and even be dangerous. About 15 per cent of patients will end up with brain damage, organ damage, memory loss, speech problems or loss of vision or hearing.

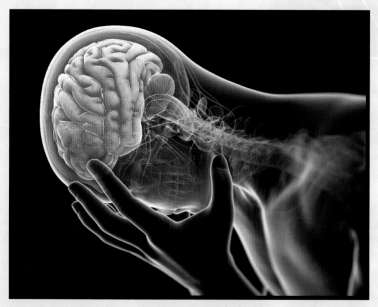

▶ A swollen brain is one of the symptoms of meningitis.

shock medical condition caused by a dangerous drop in blood pressure and flow; people suffering from shock can die

MIKE'S STORY

Mike went to hospital with bacterial meningitis. His fever reached 41°C (105.9°F). He fell into a coma. When Mike finally woke up, he could not hear. He also could not walk or lift his arms or legs. He had to be fed through a tube in his stomach.

Finally Mike was able to leave hospital. But then he needed to do special exercises to help him to sit up, stand and walk again. After several months Mike was able to walk using a walking stick. In time he was able to walk without any help. During this time he was also given implants for his ears to help him hear again.

Mike also suffers from mental after-effects of meningitis. His short-term memory is poor. He finds it difficult to make decisions. Mike is depressed about how meningitis still affects him. But he tries to have a positive attitude. He tries his best every day.

AFTER-EFFECTS OF BACTERIAL MENINGITIS

Meningitis bacteria cause the meninges to swell. The swollen tissues put pressure on the brain. This causes brain damage. It can last a short time or go on for years. It may change a person's memory, mood and behaviour. The bacteria can also damage the body's organs. This can cause many problems.

Bacteria that cause meningitis can get into a person's bloodstream. They multiply in the blood and release poisons that can destroy blood vessels. They can reduce the amount of oxygen that flows throughout the body. Without enough oxygen, the person's organs and limbs may start to die. Some people need to have damaged tissue replaced. Others may lose arms or legs because of blood poisoning.

▼ meningitis bacteria

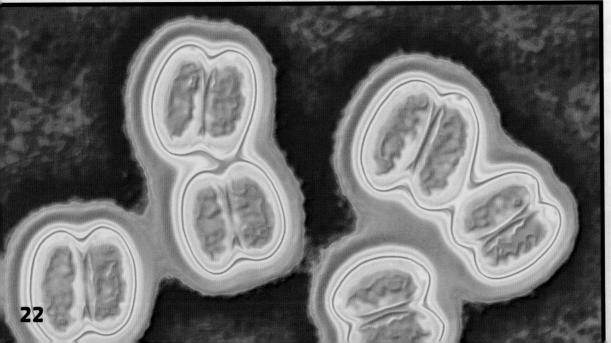

SOME POSSIBLE AFTER-EFFECTS OF BACTERIAL MENINGITIS

- balance problems
- cerebral palsy
- behavioural changes
- blindness or vision loss (temporary or permanent)
- clumsiness
- concentration problems
- deafness or hearing loss
- depression
- tiredness
- emotional changes
- epilepsy
- headaches
- sore joints or stiffness
- learning difficulties
- memory problems
- mood swings
- temper tantrums
- ringing in ears

▲ blindness

▶ headaches

CHAPTER 4

PREVENTING MENINGITIS

Anyone can get bacterial meningitis. But three things can affect your risk – your age, your lifestyle and where you live.

Infants are the most at risk for this disease. That is because their immune systems are not strong enough to fight off the disease. Teenagers and young adults are also a high-risk group. That is because the disease spreads easily in crowded places such as schools.

People who live or work closely together are at greater risk. This includes young people in the military and university students living on campus. People who travel to countries where there is an outbreak are at risk. Health-care professionals who care for meningitis patients are also at risk.

▼ university students on campus

THE MENINGITIS BELT

Developing countries are at greater risk. That is because they are often overcrowded and have unsafe water and poor health care. The highest-risk area is the Meningitis Belt in Africa. It spreads across several African countries below the Sahara Desert. The belt stretches from Senegal in the west (on the Atlantic Ocean) to Ethiopia in the east (on the Indian Ocean).

Outbreaks usually occur during Africa's dry season, from December to June. During these months the area is very dry and dusty. Many people get colds and other infections that weaken their immune systems. This increases the chances of getting meningitis.

During an outbreak one in every 1,000 people can get the disease. The largest outbreak ever recorded in Africa was in 1996–97. More than 20,000 people died. By comparison the UK has just over 3,200 cases every year in the entire country.

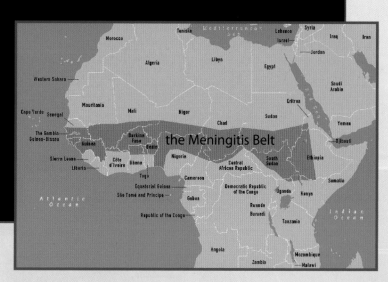

the Meningitis Belt

VACCINES

The good news is there are things you can do to lower your chances of getting meningitis. The best way is to get vaccinated. This means getting an injection that helps to protect you from the disease. No vaccine will protect you completely. But vaccines help your body to build up a defence.

▼ Vaccines help to protect against meningitis.

HEALTHY LIFESTYLE

Keeping clean is important in helping to prevent any disease. Always wash your hands before eating and after using the toilet. Regular hand-washing will help you to stay healthy.

Having a strong immune system also helps fight off disease. You can keep your immune system strong by eating healthy foods, exercising and getting enough sleep.

HEALTH FACT

Children over the age of six need at least five servings of fruit and vegetables, one hour of exercise and ten to eleven hours of sleep every day.

▼ Washing hands regularly helps to reduce the likelihood of catching diseases.

QUICK ACTION

Meningitis requires quick action. If you think you have caught the disease, tell your parents or a trusted adult and see a doctor straight away. Antibiotics may help to protect you. But you must take them as soon as possible.

▼ A doctor examines a child for meningitis.

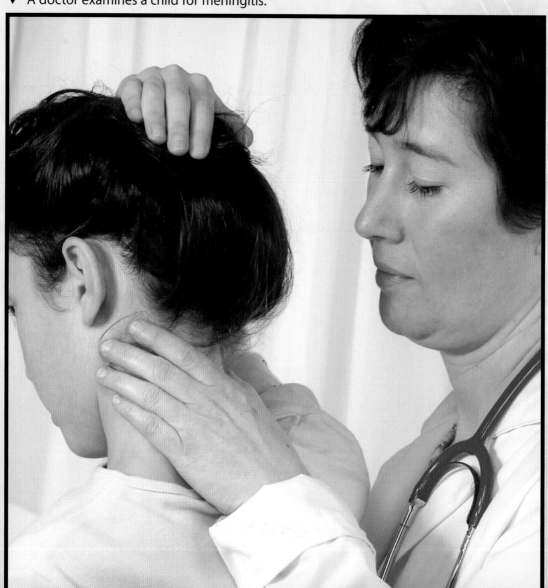

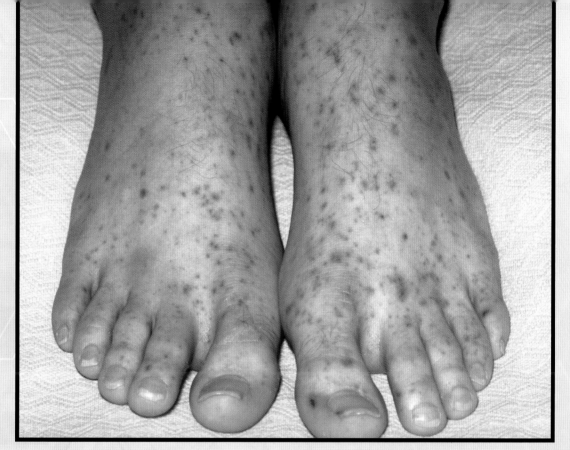

▲ meningitis body rash

Knowing what symptoms to look for could save your life. Some of the symptoms include severe headache, neck pain, fever, nausea, sleepiness and body rash. If you have most or even some of these symptoms, see a doctor straight away.

People who live in countries with access to good health care may be less likely to catch the disease. Vaccines and other medicines help people to stay healthy. But learning about this disease – and knowing what to do about it – is the best defence.

GLOSSARY

antibiotic drug that kills bacteria and is used to cure infections and disease

bacteria one-celled, microscopic living things that exist all around you and inside you; many bacteria are useful, but some cause disease

fungus single-celled organism that lives by breaking down and absorbing the natural material it lives in

immune system part of the body that protects against germs and diseases

meninges three layers of tissue that surround the brain and spinal cord

non-infectious illness or disease not caused by germs

outbreak when a number of people become ill at the same time from the same germ source

parasite animal or plant that lives on or inside another animal or plant and causes harm

seizure sudden attack of illness caused by brain swelling or other symptoms; also called a convulsion

shock medical condition caused by a dangerous drop in blood pressure and flow; people suffering from shock can die

symptom sign that suggests a person is ill or has a health problem

virus germ that infects living things and causes diseases

BOOKS

Health and Disease: From Birth to Old Age (Your Body For Life), Louise Spilsbury (Raintree, 2013)

Promoting Health and Preventing Disease (The Environment Challenge), Rebecca Vickers (Raintree, 2011)

The Usborne Complete Book of the Human Body, Anna Claybourne (Usborne, 2013)

WEBSITES

www.gosh.nhs.uk/children

The website of Great Ormond Street Hospital for Children includes lots of information about many diseases. It also provides advice about hospital stays and general health.

www.meningitis.org/symptoms/toddlers

More information and advice about the symptoms of meningitis.

INDEX

A NEW READER'S GUIDE
TO AFRICAN LITERATURE

Studies in African Literature